The Wilder Nonprofit Field Guide To

Conducting Successful Focus Groups

Judith Sharken Simon

AMHERST H.
WILDER
FOUNDATION

SAINT PAUL,
MINNESOTA

**We thank The David and Lucile Packard Foundation
and the Amherst H. Wilder Foundation for support of this publication.**

The Amherst H. Wilder Foundation is one of the largest and oldest endowed human services and community development organizations in the United States. Since 1906, the Wilder Foundation has been providing health and human services that help children and families grow strong, the elderly age with dignity, and the community grow in its ability to meet its own needs.

We hope you find this book helpful! Should you need additional information about our services, please contact:

Wilder Publishing Center
919 Lafond Avenue
Saint Paul, MN 55104
800-274-6024
www.wilder.org/pubs

The Wilder Nonprofit Field Guide series has been developed by the Wilder Publishing Center to help you and your organization find success with the daily challenges of nonprofit and community work. Other titles in this series include

Conducting Community Forums
Crafting Effective Mission and Vision Statements
Developing Effective Teams
Fundraising on the Internet

Edited by Vincent Hyman
Manufactured in the United States of America
Third printing, February 2004

Library of Congress Cataloging-in-Publication Data

Sharken Simon, Judith, date.
        The Wilder nonprofit field guide to conducting successful focus groups / Judith Sharken Simon.
            p. cm. -- (Wilder nonprofit field guide)
        Includes bibliographical references.
        ISBN 0-940069-19-9 (pbk.)
        1. Focused group interviewing. 2. Nonprofit organizations--Planning. I. Amherst H. Wilder Foundation. II. Title.
    III. Title: Conducting successful focus groups. IV. Series.
    H61.28.S53   1999
    658.4'012--dc21   99-17323

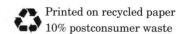

About the Author

JUDITH SHARKEN SIMON is an organization consultant who has worked with nonprofits for over fifteen years. She has led numerous data-gathering efforts involving focus groups, interviews, and surveys. In her consulting role, Judy assists clients with nonprofit organization development, including life stage transitions, strategic planning, and board development. Judy has a master's degree in organization development from the University of Minnesota and is the author of *The Five Life Stages of Nonprofit Organization: Where You Are, Where You're Going, and What to Expect When You Get There* (2001). Judy has worked extensively with the Saint Paul and Minneapolis area Southeast Asian communities. She developed and coordinated the Southeast Asian Leadership Program and has served as a consultant, supervisor, and instructor for the Bicultural Training Partnership. Judy has also been a senior consultant with Community Services Group of the Amherst H. Wilder Foundation, a project manager for a county government human services department, a mentorship coordinator in human resource development, and a public workshop trainer on focus groups and other topics related to nonprofit management. In her work, she has consulted with small, grassroots organizations and large government entities—new and old.

Contents

Introduction

Why Your Nonprofit Should Use Focus Groups

Why should your nonprofit use a focus group? After all, you're already at work doing good in the community. Aren't focus groups just for advertising firms and big businesses interested in carving out a few more percentage points of market share?

While focus groups are used in all sectors, nonprofit organizations have a unique reason to use them. Nonprofit organizations exist to serve the community. They fill in the gap that is created when market forces and government systems do not adequately address community needs. In this way, nonprofit organizations have an obligation to connect with their communities to find out what their needs are. Focus groups are an excellent way for nonprofit organizations to do this.

Focus groups are especially useful for two aspects of nonprofit management: planning of any type and service evaluation and improvement. At any point in planning—during the development of a long-term strategic plan, a marketing plan, or the plans around a specific department—focus groups are one way of collecting essential information about the opinions and interests of the community your nonprofit serves. Similarly, focus groups can uncover valuable insights on the community's present and future needs, which can help your organization evaluate and improve the quality of its services or products.

Focus groups are especially useful for two aspects of nonprofit management: planning of any type and service evaluation and improvement.

Focus groups have many benefits for nonprofits, but one is often overlooked: *Focus groups can build goodwill*. For one thing, participants usually enjoy focus groups and feel flattered when you ask for their opinions. More important, however, when people who *care* about your organization find out that their participation in a focus group has made a difference, they feel good about their involvement with you. They're likely to continue to care about and support your organization.

Beyond the connection to the community, focus groups can be an inexpensive tool for often financially strapped nonprofit organizations to gather information. While it's true that some organizations spend a lot of money on focus groups, they can also be conducted using little more than staff or volunteer time and the cost of refreshments.

The goal of this booklet is to help you and your nonprofit collect valuable information without a lot of expense, research, or specific expertise. While some researchers would argue that you need more expertise in research design to do a "quality" focus group, my experience has been that you can conduct useful focus groups that, though less sophisticated than those conducted by marketing firms, yield valuable results.

Of course, you must involve the right people, ask the right questions, and commit to follow-up action to realize the benefits of focus groups. Your position as a nonprofit serving a community means that you have a built-in group of constituents invested in (and with opinions about) your mission. A focus group can be just the thing to find out what they want.

This booklet is arranged into three sections:

> *Part I* helps you understand what a focus group is, whether a focus group is a good choice for your project, and situations in which nonprofit organizations typically use focus groups.

> *Part II* provides ten steps for conducting a focus group. You will learn how to define and plan for the focus group, how to actually conduct it, and how to interpret and translate the results into action.

> Finally, the *Appendix* includes frequently asked questions, worksheets, and samples to guide the development of your

---

The goal of this booklet is to help you and your nonprofit collect valuable information without a lot of expense, research, or specific expertise.

focus group. It also includes a list of helpful resources
should you want to know more about focus groups.

One final note before you get started. This booklet represents just
one approach to focus groups and to the larger question of how
nonprofits can collect information about the work they're doing.
Use the procedures here as a starting point, adapting them to fit
your goals and the needs of the people you serve.

Good luck and have fun!

Part I
What Is a Focus Group?

Sometimes you'll read about politicians conducting "focus groups" involving a hundred or more people. That's not what most researchers would consider a focus group; perhaps it's a helpful community forum, but it's not a focus group.

Here's a useful definition:

> A *focus group* is *"a carefully planned discussion designed to obtain perceptions on a defined area of interest in a permissive, nonthreatening environment. It is conducted with approximately seven to ten people by a skilled interviewer. The discussion is comfortable and often enjoyable for participants as they share their ideas and perceptions. Group members influence each other by responding to ideas and comments in the discussion."* [1]

So a focus group is a planned, focused discussion involving a small group of people and facilitated by an interviewer. (Don't be frightened by the word *skilled* in the definition. You may already have the skills you need. If not, you can usually find someone who does, or you can develop them yourself.)

---

[1] Richard A. Krueger, *Focus Groups: A Practical Guide for Applied Research*, 1988, page number unknown.

Just to be clear, a focus group is about people's feelings, beliefs, and perceptions. It is *not*

- A quantitative research method. In most cases, you can't attach numbers to the responses and information you collect. Rather, a focus group provides qualitative information. It relies on the words and observations of people rather than numbers.

- A brainstorming session. While focus groups do involve fluid discussion and conversation, they follow a defined format with a set of structured questions.

Focus groups are an excellent way to gather information, but they are not the only way. Interviews and written surveys are two other popular tools. As you read this booklet, give careful thought to whether a focus group is the best way to get the information you are looking for.

Some of the advantages to using a focus group are

+ It provides an opportunity for obtaining more in-depth information.

+ It offers a good means for developing survey questions.

+ It allows you to observe and record nonverbal communication that would be missed in a survey.

+ It can be conducted inexpensively.

+ The results can be gathered quickly.

+ It's a good way to hear from a wide range of constituencies.

+ It encourages the exchange of ideas between people and can generate new ideas that are less likely to be uncovered using other methods.

+ It is more personal than a survey because it brings people together in a relaxed and inviting setting.

Focus groups also have their limitations:

- A facilitator is needed to conduct the focus group.

- Because group dynamics can be difficult to control, the conversation may get diverted and issues may be raised that do not pertain to your purpose.

- Time is limited, so the number of questions that can be asked is also fairly limited.

- Assembling the people to participate in the focus group can be time consuming and challenging.
- Because the data is gathered verbally, it can be difficult to analyze and interpret.

When Should You Use a Focus Group?

Nonprofit organizations most often use focus groups in planning, marketing, or evaluation, either to improve some specific product or service or, more globally, during the development of strategic plans, vision statements, or new mission statements. Within these broader goals, focus groups have multiple applications. These include

- Collecting opinions, beliefs, and attitudes about issues of interest to your organization
- Checking out your assumptions
- Encouraging discussion about a particular topic
- Building energy, ideas, and excitement about a topic from the spontaneous combination of participants' comments
- Providing an opportunity for the facilitator and participants to learn more about a topic or issue

While all these are valuable, the first two—collecting opinions, beliefs, and attitudes on issues of interest to your organization and checking out your assumptions—are the most important.
The last three goals are sometimes reasons organizations conduct focus groups but are better thought of as welcome by-products.

Before deciding to use a focus group, give careful consideration to whether it is the best way to gather the information you need. Also consider combining the focus group method with other data-gathering methods such as interviews, surveys, or research into secondary sources such as census statistics. For example, an agency that was planning its next year's calendar of seminars on nonprofit management wanted to find out from its clients which of many workshop topics would have the greatest draw. The organization sent out a written survey to generate a list of topics and then followed up with focus groups to explore in more detail some of the topic areas.[2]

---

[2] Focus groups can also be used in the reverse of this example: The agency could have used focus groups to generate a list of topics and then conducted a survey to gauge how many potential clients were interested in each item on the list.

Here is a sample list of situations where a focus group might be appropriate:

- To identify the range of opinions on a topic
- To identify strengths and weaknesses in services and products
- To inform decisions about where to make improvements
- To identify markets for new products or services
- To identify customer or client priorities related to changes in a service or product
- To connect with and get input from clients or constituencies
- To inform policy decisions
- To meet evaluation requirements
- To educate clients about a topic and get their feedback on it
- To generate hypotheses that can be further tested quantitatively
- To stimulate new ideas about older products
- To generate ideas for new, creative concepts
- To interpret previously obtained quantitative results, such as those from a survey
- To gather data *before* beginning an activity such as planning, program design, or market research
- To gather data *during* an activity so you can make midcourse corrections
- To gather data *after* an activity so you can assess how the activity went and make changes for the next time you do it

Now that you know what a focus group is, it's time to learn how to conduct one. The rest of this booklet will help you do that.

Part II

How to Conduct a Focus Group

This section provides a step-by-step guide to focus groups. You will learn to plan the group (Steps 1 through 7 below), implement it (Step 8), and most important, act on the results (Steps 9 and 10). Here are the ten basic steps to running a focus group:

Step 1:   Define the Purpose

Step 2:   Establish a Timeline

Step 3:   Identify and Invite the Participants

Step 4:   Generate the Questions to Be Asked

Step 5:   Develop a Script

Step 6:   Select a Facilitator

Step 7:   Choose the Location

Step 8:   Conduct the Focus Group

Step 9:   Interpret and Report the Results

Step 10: Translate the Results into Action

At the end of each step you will find a ✐ **TASK**. This describes what you need to do to complete the step. In the back of the booklet you'll find worksheets and samples you can use to guide the development of your focus group.

Step 1: Define the Purpose

It is critical that you are clear *why* you are holding a focus group. A clear purpose will help you

- Get the information you need
- Develop focused questions
- Communicate to the participants why you are conducting a focus group

The purpose statement for the focus group answers the question, "What do we want to achieve by gathering data using a focus group?" A good focus group purpose statement is focused and specific. Purpose statements that are broad and general, such as "To find out what people think," make it difficult to identify participants, develop questions, and get useful results.

The clearer the purpose statement, the easier the design of the rest of the focus group.

To develop a clear purpose statement for your focus group, write an initial purpose statement. Then ask, "Why do we want to know that?" Usually the answer will reveal a clearer and more refined purpose statement. The clearer the purpose statement, the easier the design of the rest of the focus group.

Below are some examples of focus group purpose statements.

Example 1

A community education program is planning next year's courses and wants to know if it is offering enough daytime classes.

Focus group purpose statement: To find out from community residents their perceptions and ideas about our daytime programming.

Example 2

A mental health agency has greatly expanded its services and wants to revise its mission statement.

Focus group purpose statement: To hear how our constituents perceive and describe our services and to use that information to help us revise our mission statement.

Example 3

A county government is developing a new policy related to its employee benefits and wants to get staff reaction to the draft policy before finalizing it.

Focus group purpose statement: To describe the new employee benefits policy, find out how staff members feel about it, and write it in language the staff will understand.

Turn to Worksheet 1: Purpose Statement, on page 45. Use the questions there to develop a purpose statement that will guide the development of your focus group questions.

TASK

Step 2: Establish a Timeline

As with most things in life, running a focus group cannot be done overnight. At minimum, you should start planning for your focus group at *least* four weeks ahead of the actual focus group session date. Six to eight weeks is probably more realistic. It takes time to identify the participants, develop and test the questions, locate a site, invite and follow up with participants, and gather the materials for the sessions. You must have all the pieces in place if you are going to have a successful focus group. Below is a list of standard components and a typical timeline:

Timeline Components	Time Frame
1. Write the focus group purpose statement	6–8 weeks prior to the session date
2. Identify the participants	6–8 weeks prior
3. Gather address and phone information on the participants	6–8 weeks prior
4. Select a facilitator	4–5 weeks prior
5. Develop the questions	4–5 weeks prior
6. Develop a script	4–5 weeks prior
7. Arrange and reserve the session site	4 weeks prior
8. Write and send the invitations	3–4 weeks prior

Timeline Components	Time Frame
9. Follow up the invitations with phone calls	2 weeks prior
10. Make room arrangements (seating, equipment, refreshments, and so forth)	1 week prior
11. Place a reminder call to the participants	2 days prior
12. Gather session materials	2 days prior
13. Conduct the focus group	Session date
14. Send a thank-you letter to the participants	2 days post
15. Transcribe the notes from the session	2 days post
16. Summarize the session and mail summary to the participants	1 week post
17. Analyze sessions and write report	When all information is gathered

TASK   *Complete Worksheet 2: Focus Group Timeline, on page 47, to make sure you have all the critical components covered.*

Step 3: Identify and Invite the Participants

You have developed the purpose statement and written a timeline for your focus groups. The next step is to identify who will participate. Deciding who to invite is really a five-step process:

1. Decide how many participants you need and how many you'll need to invite.

2. Review your focus group purpose statement and develop a list of key attributes to seek in the focus group participants.

3. Brainstorm possible participants and categories of participants using the list of attributes you developed.

4. Refine the list by using the "two characteristics in common" and the "homogeneity and heterogeneity" guidelines provided on page 18.

5. Secure names and contact information, finalize the list, and send invitations.

1. Decide how many participants you need and how many you'll need to invite.

Before you decide who to invite, it's good to have a figure in mind for the number of actual participants you need. This number is a function of the number of focus groups you plan to hold, the number of participants you want in each group, and the likely response rate you expect to your invitations. Sounds complicated, but it's not. Here are some simple rules to help you figure this all out.

Number of focus groups: To some degree, the number of focus groups you hold is shaped by the resources (staff, time, and money) you have. Beyond a resource limitation, you need to conduct enough focus groups to get a handle on the information you are trying to gather. As you decide which constituents to contact, ask yourself, "Are these the people we need information from to make the right decisions?" If you are collecting information on many questions from many constituent audiences, you will need more focus groups than if you seek information on a few specific programs from a few audiences. We have found that most major themes and patterns emerge within three sessions with any one type of audience. Therefore, three focus groups with any particular audience is a starting rule for how many sessions to hold.

> We have found that most major themes and patterns emerge within three sessions with any one type of audience.

The number of focus groups should be shaped by the ultimate purpose. Consider the example of a transitional housing agency that wanted to evaluate its services at a site that served three distinct groups: elderly people, women with young children, and recent Somali immigrants. The agency had two options: it could have held three focus groups with a mixed attendance from all three types, or it could have held three separate focus groups with *each* of these populations, a total of nine groups. The agency had limited resources, and it was more interested in the opinions from its clients as a whole, so the planning team decided to hold only three groups, each consisting of representatives from all three of these categories. Note, though, that if the purpose of the focus group had been to determine *specifically* what elderly people, Somali immigrants, and women with children thought of the services, then as many as three separate focus groups with *each* specific group would be warranted.

Communication barriers, cultural differences, or access to the participants could also have shaped the number of focus groups.

There are other reasons to have more than three focus groups for each type of audience. For example, a drug abuse prevention organization in the midst of strategic planning decided to get staff input into the strengths and weaknesses of its vision statement. The facilitator, at the request of the planning group, arranged seven focus groups involving all staff members. After the third focus group, the facilitator reported hearing similar information. The planning team wanted all staff to feel they had the opportunity to speak, so it instructed the facilitator to complete the remaining sessions even though it was probable little new information would emerge.

After determining the number of focus groups, you should determine the size of each group.

Group size: Focus groups should be kept to six to twelve participants. Fewer than six participants tends to limit the conversation, because there is not enough diversity to spark energy and creativity. More than twelve participants gets unwieldy, because voices get lost. Determine how many people you expect to be in each focus group. If you have less than six, consider expanding your criteria, combining two groups of people, or both. If you discover your group will be larger than twelve, consider holding more than one focus group or narrowing your criteria.

Having determined the number of participants in each group, you next need to estimate how many people will respond to your invitations.

Response rate: In most focus groups, the participants are selected and invited to participate. If participants come from a preexisting group, such as the people at a regularly scheduled staff meeting, then attendance and how many to invite is not an issue—response rate will be close to 100 percent. When participants are *not* part of some regular meeting, the general rule is to invite one and one-half to two times as many people as you want to come. (This means you expect a response rate of 66 percent to 50 percent.) For a focus group of six to twelve this means inviting between nine and twenty-four participants. If you use a group that's harder to reach, such as single parents or homeless people, you may need to adjust your expected response rate to a lower percentage. You may also need to make accommodations, such as providing child care, transportation, or meals, to raise the response rate.

The formula for figuring the number of people to invite is based on the number of groups, the group size, and the predicted response rate, and it looks like this:

(number of focus groups) × *(number of participants per group)* ÷ *(response rate)* = *number of invitations*

For example, if you intend to hold three groups of ten participants each and you expect that about 66 percent of the people you invite will respond, the formula is

(3 groups) × *(10 people per group)* ÷ *(0.66)* = *45 invitations*

After you've figured out how many people you need to invite, you can begin deciding who to invite.

2. Review your focus group purpose statement and develop a list of key attributes to seek in participants.

Rarely do you want to conduct a focus group with just *any* living human. You need to develop a list of attributes to guide your selection of participants. Derive these attributes from words in your focus group purpose statement that indicate important participant characteristics. Although the attributes you base your selection on depend solely on your focus group purpose statement, here are some attributes typically considered when brainstorming possible participants:

- Age
- Areas of expertise (child care, public health, theater)
- Employment status
- Family size
- Gender
- Geographic location (neighborhood, proximity to service, work site)
- Income
- Past experience with product or service
- Race or ethnicity (or both)
- Relationship to the organization (donor, client, volunteer)
- Sector affiliation (business, nonprofit, foundation, government)
- Tenure (with the agency, in the neighborhood)

For example, a low-income housing development group might find that its purpose statement includes key words such as *neighborhood resident* (location), *culturally diverse* (ethnicity and race), and *household income less than $27,000* (income). It will use these words as guides when it begins brainstorming people to invite. (Further examples of this process follow shortly.)

3. Brainstorm possible participants and categories of participants.

After defining some basic attributes, brainstorm possible participants who have these attributes. The list you develop can include both names of individuals as well as categories of individuals. In the housing example above, both *Alex Lee* and *families whose children use the local school meal subsidy program* appear on the list.

Brainstorming simply means generating a list of people (or categories of people) to attend the focus group. Whether done by a team or an individual, the main point in brainstorming is to keep the ideas flowing. Therefore, avoid critiquing any item on the list until all ideas have been noted. Then you can go back and narrow the list based on the goals of your research and the attributes you have selected.

Let's revisit the purpose statement examples from Step 1 (pages 10–11) to see how three agencies generated possible participants.

Example 1

A community education program is planning next year's courses and wants to know if it is offering enough daytime classes.

Focus group purpose statement: To find out from community residents their perceptions and ideas about our daytime programming.

Key words: residents, daytime, community

Possible focus group participants:

- Residents within a five-mile radius of the community school site

- Past participants of daytime programs

- Members of a nearby church daytime book club

Example 2

A mental health agency has greatly expanded its services and wants to revise its mission statement.

Focus group purpose statement: To hear how our constituents perceive and describe our services and use that information to help us revise our mission statement.

Key words: constituents, perceptions of services

Possible focus group participants:

- Members of one or more of the agency's support groups

- Funders

- Related service providers

Example 3

A county government is developing a new policy related to its employee benefits and wants to get staff reaction to the draft policy before finalizing it.

Focus group purpose statement: To convey the new employee benefits policy, find out how staff feel about it, and write it in language staff will understand.

Key words: staff, benefits

Possible focus group participants:

- Staff who are enrolled in the agency's benefits plan

- Staff who have voiced dissatisfaction with the benefits plan

- Staff who have voiced dissatisfaction with the agency's policies

- Staff who are eligible for benefits

- All staff

It's easy to see from these examples how the focus group planners moved from the purpose statement to a few key words to some categories of possible participants. The next step is to refine the list.

4. Refine the list by using the "two characteristics in common" and the "homogeneity and heterogeneity" guidelines.

You need the right mix of people to elicit the synergy that makes focus groups so useful. To do this, balance the commonalities and differences in participants; select for enough diversity to stimulate opinions and enough similarity to create a common ground. The following guidelines can help you find the right mix.

> *Two characteristics in common*: Participants should have at least two factors in common. In example 1 on page 16, you might limit the selection to people who have participated in a daytime program *and* who live within five miles of the community school site.

> *Homogeneity and heterogeneity:* After deciding on two factors in common, you need to ensure some variety among participants, but not so much that you trigger conflict. In the above example, you would not want participants who all went to the same daytime session and live in the 700 block of Hilly Road. Conversely, you would avoid inviting participants whose views or experiences are so disparate that the information will be distorted, tension will arise, or outright conflict will occur. In the example above, this might mean that you'd avoid mixing people from an extremely impoverished part of the district with those who live in luxury. Other examples of a poor mix: inviting staff and management to the same focus group to comment on the agency's management style or inviting alumni of fifty years and new students to the same focus group on a university's core values.

Now that you've got a clear picture of what the group participants should be like, it's time to name the individuals you'll invite and send them invitations.

5. Secure names and contact information, finalize the list, and send invitations.

If the group you've identified is not preexisting (such as a staff group, museum members, or the tenants of a particular building), you must figure out how to build an invitation list. Here are a few suggestions:

- Use an existing list related to your attribute list. Examples of existing lists include your donors, your employees, a county or city database, a complementary agency's client list, or a subscription list to a local publication that reaches your target audience.

- Purchase or borrow someone else's list and randomly select names from it. (For example, select every fifth person on the list.)

- Recruit on site. For example, ask the first thirty registrants at a conference if they would be interested in participating in a focus group.

- Show colleagues your categories and ask for names.

For example, if you are looking for participants who are more than seventy years old, you might ask a nearby senior center to lend you their list of participants. If you want homeowners, you might get a list from block clubs in the geographic area you are targeting. If you want people who use food shelves, you could recruit on site at local food shelves. If you want nonprofit directors with expertise in diversity training, you could ask colleagues for suggestions from their professional networks.

Be sure your list includes names, correct salutations, addresses, and phone numbers. Depending on the size of the lists you develop and the number of participants you are hoping for, you might use the entire list or a random sample, choosing every second or third person on the list.

Once you've got the list, it's time to send out invitations and make plans for follow-up phone calls to remind participants. A sample invitation letter is provided on page 51.

TASK

Turn to Worksheet 3: Participant List, page 49, to complete this step.

Step 4: Generate the Questions to Be Asked

The particular questions posed in a focus group are critical. Because of the length of the focus group (usually one to two hours), there is time for four to five questions. That's not many, especially when you consider that there are really two kinds of questions: introductory or warm-up questions and more serious questions that get at the heart of your research. Since the first two questions are usually a warm-up of some sort, that leaves you three questions to probe the issue you're researching.

The sequence and tone of the questions are as significant as the questions themselves. To be effective, focus group questions should

- Be open-ended[3]
- Be focused
- Move from the general to the specific

Here are some examples of ineffective and effective questions.

Ineffective	Effective
Do you like the work we do? (This is closed-ended and elicits a "yes" or "no" response.)	What do you consider to be our strengths? (This is open-ended; it encourages people to think and respond at length.)
What do you like best about the proposed strategic plan? (This is too general. It should focus on a specific point.)	What do you like best about how the strategic plan is being communicated? (This is focused; it attends to the way the plan is communicated.)
Why do you refuse to use our services? (This questions is too abrupt. Some participants may feel defensive or uncomfortable giving criticism, so you should ease the participants into discussions of negative issues.)	1. What are some of our strengths? 2. In what areas could we improve? 3. What about our services do you really dislike? (This series of questions moves the participants to a point where they feel more comfortable expressing criticisms. It also moves smoothly from general to specific issues.)

---

[3] There *is* an exception to this: Closed-ended questions can be very helpful during the warm-up stage. For example, you can ask everyone to rate the organization on a scale of one to five, or how many people have more than three years experience with the organization, or how many people live outside the neighborhood. The responses to these questions usually won't help analysis in any concrete way. But such questions are easy to answer and help the participants feel comfortable speaking in the group.

When designing questions, you may find the following process helpful.

1. Either alone or with a group of people, brainstorm a list of possible questions.

2. Prioritize, rewrite, and sequence the questions.

3. Test the questions and refine as needed.

1. Brainstorm questions.

When brainstorming questions, revisit your purpose statement. Generate a list of questions you'd like to ask in relation to that statement. Remember, one of the cardinal rules of brainstorming is that you are not to critique or judge the questions while generating the list. Quantity, rather than quality, is the primary goal.

For example, the community education program whose focus group purpose statement was "To find out from community residents their perceptions and ideas about our daytime programming" brainstormed the following questions:

- What do you like about our daytime programs?

- Which of our daytime programs have you attended?

- What kind of daytime programs would you be interested in attending?

- What do you wish could be improved about our daytime programs?

- What activities do you engage in during your leisure time?

- What kinds of classes have you taken in the past?

- What are some of the things you look for when choosing a class?

- What are some of the things you look for when choosing a daytime class?

- How do you decide whether to take a daytime class?

- If we were offering the ideal schedule of daytime classes, what would it include or look like?

- What advice would you give us about our daytime classes?

- What changes would you make in our daytime programs?

- Are there some evening programs you wish were offered during the day?

- Why do you choose not to attend daytime classes?

2. Prioritize, rewrite, and sequence the questions.

Once you have a list of questions, look at your purpose statement once again. Which questions do not apply? Which questions seem really important? Now look at your possible participants. Which questions would they be able to respond to? Eliminate as many questions as you can. If you are using a group to design the questions, have everyone vote for their top five questions from the whole list. Those questions with the most votes "win." Once you have selected the top five or six questions, find someone with good editing skills to rewrite them. Finally, arrange the questions in a sequence that will be comfortable for the participants, moving from the general to the specific, easy to challenging, and positive to negative.

3. Test the questions and refine as needed.

Before using the questions in an actual focus group session, test them out. Do the responses you get give you the information you need? On paper, our questions often seem great, but when implemented they don't elicit the responses we need. Go through the questions yourself and try answering them as if you were in the focus group. Pull some staff members together for a practice focus group and try the questions on them. If they work, use them. If not, revise them.

For examples of final focus group questions, see the sample script for Teen Safe on page 55.

TASK   *Develop a list of questions following the instructions above. Fill them in on Worksheet 4: Focus Group Questions, page 53.*

Step 5: Develop a Script

Generating the questions is the precursor to developing a more detailed script for your focus group. If you are experienced at running meetings, you may be tempted to do without a script. A script has several advantages, however:

- The process of writing a script helps you be sure you've put the questions in context for the participants.

- A script ensures that each focus group is conducted in a similar fashion, making the results more reliable.

- A script helps the facilitator stay on track and on time.

- A script is helpful when the facilitator is external to the process, such as a volunteer or hired facilitator.

Plan on a one- to two-hour time frame. A minimum of one hour is recommended because the process requires some time for opening and closing remarks as well as at least one or two questions. Be cautious *not to exceed two hours*. Beyond two hours participants and facilitator start to fade; the questions and subsequent discussion lose their relevance. Since the adult attention span is about twenty minutes, a good focus group script writer carefully crafts the time so that participants stay engaged, making sure sections are no more than twenty minutes long.

There are three parts to a focus group script:

1. The opening

2. The questions

3. The closing

The *opening* is the time for the facilitator to welcome the group, introduce the purpose and context of the focus group, explain what a focus group is and how it will flow, and facilitate introductions. Here is an example of the opening section of a focus group script:

> Welcome to the group and thank you for joining us. This is one of a series of focus groups that are being conducted to gather information for Teen Safe's strategic planning process. The planning team members hope that by understanding your thoughts about Teen Safe, they can improve their plans.
>
> A focus group enables people to come together in one place to share their opinions on a topic. Each of you is representing your own opinions; you do not need to view your comments as representative of an organization or a group of people. Please be as honest and open as possible in your responses. Your anonymity will be protected. No one at Teen Safe will know who said what. The results of the focus group will help Teen Safe plan for the future. We will move quickly through a series of questions and should be done in about an hour and a half. Let's start by introducing ourselves.

The *question* section is where you ask the questions that you designed and tested in Step 4. Below is an example of a set of questions used in a focus group script:

> 1. Please comment on how valuable Teen Safe has been in the community using the following scale[4]:
>
>   • Very valuable   • Of little value
>   • Somewhat valuable   • Of no value
>
> 2. What are some specific things about Teen Safe that you think are going well and definitely should be carried into the future?
>
> 3. What are some specific things about Teen Safe that you think could be improved in the future?
>
> 4. If you had to select the four most important areas of improvement to focus on from the entire list that was just generated, which ones would you choose?
>
> 5. What are the major barriers to making these improvements?

The *closing* section wraps up the focus group. This includes thanking the participants, giving them an opportunity and avenue for further input, telling them how the data will be used, and explaining when the larger process will be completed. Below is an example of the closing section of a focus group script:

> Please take out a sheet of paper and note any last thoughts, comments, or anything else you wish to emphasize for the planning team. You may also call me or any one of the planning team members at 555-4321 [post phone numbers on flip chart] with comments. Thank you again for your participation. You will receive a summary of this session in the mail. All of the information from this and other focus groups will be reviewed next month and summarized for a planning retreat scheduled for the end of next month. Teen Safe hopes to have a new strategic plan by the beginning of the fiscal year.

TASK

The complete sample focus group script for Teen Safe can be found on pages 55–57. Using that script as a model, write your own script using the questions you developed in Step 4.

---

[4] This is an example of how a rating scale can be used as a warm-up question, as discussed in the footnote on page 20.

Step 6: Select a Facilitator

One of the distinctions of focus groups versus interviews or written surveys is that they require a facilitator with some skill to run them. Don't be scared off by this requirement. It doesn't mean you need a highly paid consultant, but it *does* mean you need someone with a working knowledge of group dynamics and a reputation as a good meeting leader. In particular, a focus group facilitator should be able to deal tactfully with outspoken group members, keep the discussion on track, and make sure every participant is heard. The job description for the facilitator includes

- Setting the tone so that participants have fun and feel good about the session

- Making sure every participant is heard

- Getting full answers by probing for more information

- Monitoring the time

- Keeping the discussion on track

- Heading off exchanges of opinion about individual items

- Ensuring that the written comments can be understood by the person who interprets the results (if other than the facilitator)

More information on each of these duties is provided in Step 8.

Finding a facilitator is not difficult. The facilitator can be a staff member, volunteer, or member of a committee or task force. Budget permitting, you can hire a professional facilitator. You can also use a two-person team, where one person moderates the discussion and another records it.

Be wary of any qualities of the facilitator (or facilitators) that might make participants uncomfortable. For example, you may not want the organization's executive director to facilitate a staff focus group about a new performance appraisal system.

Also consider qualities that might make participants more comfortable. For example, a facilitator from outside the organization may be viewed as more objective and may elicit more honest responses from participants.

Choose a facilitator. Familiarize this person with your plan, your work to date, and the script you've developed. The facilitator may have helpful revisions or adjustments to these items.

 TASK

Step 7: Choose the Location

You don't need a room with a one-way mirror or sophisticated recording devices for a focus group, but you do need a setting in which the participants feel comfortable expressing their opinions.

Some of the factors to consider when choosing a location are

- What message does the setting send? (Is it corporate, upscale, cozy, informal, sterile, inviting?)
- Does the setting encourage conversation?
- How will the setting affect the information gathered? Will the setting bias the information offered?
- Can it comfortably accommodate nine to fifteen people (six to twelve participants plus facilitators), where all can view each other?
- Is it easily accessible? (Consider access for people with disabilities, safety, transportation, parking, proximity, and convenience.)

Choose a setting that makes the participants comfortable, whether at your office or some other location. For example, if you are conducting a focus group with members of a mutual support group, you may want to hold the session at the support group's regular meeting place. It is a familiar setting for them and can accommodate the other focus group logistics easily. If you are conducting a focus group of funders, it may be beneficial to hold the session at one of your board member's corporate board-rooms—a setting that may be more familiar to the funders. The key is to be a good host, putting your participants' comfort first.

TASK   *Identify and reserve a location that will be comfortable and convenient for participants.*

Step 8: Conduct the Focus Group

Now that you've identified why you're doing a focus group, selected and invited the participants, chosen the facilitator and location, and developed the script, it's time to actually conduct the session.

The materials you will need for the session are:

- Extra notepads and pencils
- Flip chart or easel paper
- Focus group script
- List of participants and their phone numbers
- Markers

- Masking tape
- Name tags
- Refreshments
- Tape recorder (optional)
- Watch or clock

Conducting the focus group is a matter of following the script, but of course there's more to it. The facilitator should arrive before the participants, set out the refreshments, and arrange the room so all participants can view one another; U-shaped seating or all at one table is best. As participants arrive, the facilitator should set the tone for a comfortable, enjoyable discussion by welcoming them as would any gracious host.

Once the group gets underway, all the skills of a good facilitator come into play. Think of it as a combination of running a meeting and managing group dynamics. Attention to the following items will help ensure success:

1. Set the tone: Participants should have fun and feel good about the session.

2. Make sure every participant is heard.

3. Get full answers (not just "we need more money" but "we need more money to hire a receptionist to answer phones").

4. Monitor time closely.

5. Keep the discussion on track.

6. Head off exchanges of opinion about individual items.

1. Set the tone.

Most people enjoy an opportunity to voice their opinions and share ideas with others. A good facilitator fosters an atmosphere of comfort, enjoyment, and the open exchange of ideas. Here is a list of ways to set an appropriate tone:

- Offer snacks and drinks.
- Have appropriate and comfortable seating, writing surfaces, and lighting.
- Greet the participants.
- Introduce the participants to each other.
- Explain that the comments collected will not be attributed to any specific individual, so they can speak freely.
- Thank the participants for attending.

2. Make sure every participant is heard.

After careful consideration of who to invite, the last thing you want is to miss someone's input because of shyness or domineering participants. Try these techniques to make sure that every participant is heard:

- Ask people to write down their thoughts before speaking.
- Ask people to respond one by one in a specific order.
- Directly ask the more dominant participants to hold back.
- Instruct participants to work in pairs and report their discussion.

3. Get full answers.

Many participants are not used to sharing their thoughts aloud in a group setting and may offer quite brief responses. Also, many participants assume that their response adequately describes their entire thought. The facilitator must take care to probe for more comprehensive responses. Detailed information will help those analyzing the focus group summaries get more of a flavor for the sentiments and opinions of the participants. Some common probes to get more in-depth information are

- Can you tell me more?
- What specifically do you mean by that?

- Is there anything else?

- Can you share an example of what you've mentioned?

4. Monitor time closely.

Attending the focus group is an additional commitment the participants voluntarily make; don't waste their time. A well-planned, detailed script is useful because it defines how much time is needed and allotted for each part of the focus group session. Stick to the agenda and get people in and out of the session on time. Bring a watch or clock and use it.

5. Keep the discussion on track.

Since the value of focus groups is the synergy of discussion, it's easy for the discussion to synergize into a completely different topic. Experienced facilitators have a variety of techniques for herding discussions gone astray. Here are some:

- State that the discussion seems to have wandered; then refocus the participants on the topic at hand.

- Rephrase or reframe the strayed discussion in terms pertinent to the current topic.

- Move on to the next question.

- If it is a particular participant who seems to be taking the group off track, take a short break, take that person aside, and gently ask him or her to stick to the topic at hand.

6. Head off exchanges of opinion about individual items.

A focus group is not a forum for arguments and public speeches, so the facilitator must steer conversation away from either of those fatalities. Facilitator comments such as the following will help avoid confrontations between participants:

- "Both opinions are valid. I'll make sure to note *both* of them."

- "We are here to capture *everyone's* thoughts. Let's make sure I have them all."

- "The purpose here is to gather information. We do not need to resolve anything. I will make sure to note your thoughts."

- "I suggest we move on."

- "If you have further ideas or thoughts please make a note of them, and I'll make sure to include them in the focus group summary."

Attending the focus group is an additional commitment the participants voluntarily make; don't waste their time.

Facilitating a focus group can be daunting, especially the first time. To help guide the process, create a detail sheet that summarizes the goals of the focus group, the names of participants, materials required, and so forth. Worksheet 5: Focus Group Details Sheet, on page 59 can help you do this.

TASK

Use Worksheet 5: Focus Group Details Sheet, page 59, to create a detail sheet for the focus group. Then conduct the focus group.

Step 9: Interpret and Report the Results

The focus group will be of little use without a report on it. There are really three steps to creating such a report:

1. Summarize each meeting *immediately* after it ends.

2. Analyze the summaries.

3. Write the report.

1. Summarize each meeting.

After *each* session there are a number of details to attend to.

- If you've taped the meeting, be sure to spot-check the tape. If there was some failure, it's easier to reconstruct the discussion immediately after the session.

- The facilitator should review the session with another person to capture fresh impressions.

(A facilitator summary sheet is helpful for these first two items. See Worksheet 6: Facilitator Summary Sheet, page 61.)

- Finally, transcribe notes that were taken soon after the session is over and write a summary of the focus group. (See Sample Focus Group Summary on page 63.) The quick turnaround time on the transcription helps avoid memory lapses. It's easiest for the facilitator or recorder to remember what was meant by a particular acronym or shorthand immediately following the session than it is a month later.

Summaries have two uses. First, you need them when you analyze the data. Second, you can send the summary to the participants as a tangible product. By sending them the summary you engage them more fully in your process; they have a chance to correct any mistakes or misrepresentations, they see that the data was in fact captured, and they are able to see in writing their group's total comments, which may help them to understand conclusions that may be drawn from the focus groups. Moreover, the extra contact with the participants increases your opportunities to help them feel connected to your organization.

2. Analyze the summaries.

After completing all the focus groups and focus group summaries, it's time to group the results and analyze them. Start by reading all the focus group summaries in one sitting, noting trends and surprises. As you look for these elements, keep in mind that context and tone are equal in importance to the reiteration of particular words. If a comment (or number of comments) seemed to be phrased negatively, elicited emotional responses, or seemed to trigger many other comments, that would be worth noting in the analysis.

Trends are comments that seem to appear repeatedly in the data. For example, if you are reviewing summaries from five focus groups about the agency's image and each one of them had a number of comments using the word *content experts*, that's a clear trend. This trend should be reported, as it is something the agency may want to build on or change, depending on its goals.

Surprises are unexpected comments that are worth noting. For example, one agency conducted a series of focus groups as a way to gather information for a new marketing campaign. The agency had heard that some people felt it was aloof, inaccessible, or out of touch with the residents in areas where it had branch offices. It wanted to be perceived as a friend and resource to these communities. In one focus group summary, the follow-up team noticed a comment related to the fact that all the organization's offices were at the summits of hills. This was a surprising and helpful comment. It was new information that clarified at least one aspect of the agency's image with its neighbors.

Trends are comments that seem to appear repeatedly in the data.

Surprises are unexpected comments that are worth noting.

3. Write the report.

The final report can take many different shapes but should include these elements:

    I. Background and purpose of the report

   II. Details of the sessions

- Number of focus groups conducted.
- Name of facilitator.
- Dates of sessions.
- Identifying information about each focus group, including participant characteristics and the number of people in each session. Be sure not to attribute statements to particular individuals and, when information is sensitive, do not reveal names at all.

  III. Results

- Trends.
- Surprises.
- Quotes that represent a diversity of comments and show typical comments.

  IV. Conclusions

   V. Appendix (optional): focus group script or list of questions

When writing up the results, review the purpose statement and consider the audience for the report. This check back to the "beginning" often helps focus the report. For example, a child care resource center was doing a focus group of staff as part of its strategic planning process. The purpose of the focus group was to determine strengths and weaknesses of the organization. The results of the focus groups were going to be reported to the strategic planning committee, which consisted of the agency's managers and some board members. The staff made many statements indicating a lack of management skills at the agency. Because of the audience, the final report had to tactfully emphasize the need for management skill-building as part of the agency's strategic plan.

TASK

Summarize each focus group, using as guides Worksheet 6: Facilitator Summary Sheet, on page 61 and the Sample Focus Group Summary on page 63. Then gather all the focus group summaries and write the final report. Use the model above and the Sample Final Report provided on pages 65–67 to guide your work.

Step 10: Translate the Results into Action

The greatest failure in the use of focus groups is that the information is not used. This failure occurs in two areas: failure to report to the focus group participants and failure to apply the results to the purpose for which they were originally commissioned.

Remember, one benefit of focus groups for nonprofits is that the process engages people in the topic. Once they are invested, don't let them down. Follow up with participants. Mail them the summary from their session, send them a thank-you letter, and include them in correspondence about how the information was used. While good public relations is not the primary goal of a focus group, don't let the energy you invested go to waste.

Here are some tips for translating the results into action:

- Schedule a meeting to review the summaries and discuss their implications.

- Put the focus group information in context. Refer to your purpose statement and analyze the answers or insights the focus groups gave you. Compare, contrast, and combine the focus group information with information gathered from other sources such as surveys, interviews, or secondary research sources.

- Highlight the main themes, issues, problems, or questions that arose in the focus groups. Discuss and record how you will address these.

- If there is a lot of information, group it and engage an action team in a process of prioritizing it. Then decide what actions need to be taken related to the priority items. For example, share the information with local policy makers, build some items into staff work plans, and incorporate specific suggestions into the budget.

> The greatest failure in the use of focus groups is that the information is not used.

Here are examples of how two organizations translated focus group results into action:

A Hmong Violence Prevention Project was established in Minnesota to curb the rising violence-related incidents in the Southeast Asian Hmong communities. The project coordinator conducted twenty-five focus groups over the course of eight months. A twenty-page report was generated that identified the community's perceptions of violence and recommended action steps. The recommendations were sent to community leaders, funders, community agency leaders, and public officials for action. The project coordinator's job expanded to include regular contacts with those leaders, checking on (and motivating) their progress.

A public access radio station was developing a new strategic plan. It conducted three focus groups with regular listeners as part of its data-gathering step in the strategic planning process. The focus group facilitator sought information related to the strengths, weaknesses, opportunities, and threats facing the station. The focus groups, in combination with other data gathered during the planning process, helped the station identify serious critical issues standing in the way of its success. The agency's final plan included specific changes—including budget reallocations, increased fundraising, changes in program emphasis, and increased community involvement—directed at those critical issues.

Focus groups can really energize a nonprofit organization. Don't disregard the information you've collected or you'll lose the momentum that's generated when you convene people and gather their opinions. Mobilize your staff and board to help you turn the results you've collected into concrete actions.

Now, Go Get Results!

While focus groups are often seen as a technique reserved for corporations involved in expensive, competitive advertising, they are extremely useful for nonprofit organizations wishing to connect with their communities. Just as important for the budget-wise nonprofit, focus groups are relatively inexpensive and easy to conduct. Most people *love* to be asked their opinion and are generally not shy about voicing it.

As a nonprofit, you are obligated to serve and represent some group. Often it is an underrepresented, underserved community. Why not get their opinions and input through a focus group?

You'll gain valuable information and build good rapport in the process. You'll find ways to be more responsive, and you'll expand the number of people who care about and support your mission.

Now, go get results!

Appendix

Frequently Asked Questions

Here is a list of questions that often come up during workshops on focus groups.

Should we have people such as board members or staff observing the focus group?

A few observers are fine and do not interfere with the focus group. In fact, I often recommend that key staff or board members come to the focus group as observers so they can hear firsthand what participants are saying. Be careful to consider whether the observers' presence will inhibit the participants from speaking freely. For example, you wouldn't want a foundation's program officer observing a focus group of grantees. Also, be sure the number of observers isn't out of balance with the number of participants.

I've heard that it's important to pay people for attending focus groups. How does this work for financially strapped nonprofits?

It is nice to offer people a gift or token for participating in a focus group, but it is not necessary. People like to be asked their opinion and are happy to participate without an incentive. If you are able, offer an inexpensive gift related to your agency, such as a T-shirt or coffee mug imprinted with your agency's logo.

Some audiences, like parents, are especially hard to reach. How can we get them to attend a focus group?

When you expect low turnout, consider ways to minimize the barriers to attendance. For example, you can offer on-site child care, reimbursement for travel, or free bus passes. You can hold the focus group in someone's home, invite participants to bring a friend, or take the focus group to a location where the audience usually convenes. In some cases, you may need to pay people to attend, offer a meal as part of the reward for participation, or provide some other incentive that fits the needs of your audience.

Is it important to send out background information ahead of time to the focus group participants?

This depends on the purpose of the focus group. Sometimes the topic is so complex that background reading can help orient the participants. Be aware, though, that no matter what you send, some people simply won't read the information. *Never* assume that participants have read the background information you've sent them. Some nonprofits also use the focus group invitation as an opportunity for low-cost public relations by including a brochure along with the invitation.

Is it appropriate to have a board member or staff person do the opening remarks?

Absolutely. It's a great way for them to get involved, and they may even stay on as observers. I sometimes ask for an organization representative to make the opening remarks, both to extend a personal welcome and thanks to the participants and to put the focus group into context for the participants. Remember to consider whether the representative's presence will inhibit the participants in any way.

Should we record or videotape the sessions? Does recording inhibit the participants?

Recording is not necessary. First, consider whether you will review or transcribe the hours of tape. Most nonprofits that record focus groups never listen to or look at the tapes. Second, recording is one more thing to tend to. You've got to make sure the equipment is functioning and you may need someone there to operate it.

If you do decide to record the sessions, you'll find that participants are not inhibited by the equipment. They generally forget it's there within the first five minutes.

How do you do a focus group with culturally diverse groups,
particularly those with limited English?

First, consider whether a focus group is even appropriate for
the audience. For example, in working with a Cambodian
agency, we found that the concept of a focus group—a group
meeting with free-flowing discussion—was foreign to the
participants. We had limited results, even when a native
speaker facilitated the group.

Assuming the methodology is suitable for the audience,
arrange for a native speaker (or at least an interpreter) to
conduct the focus group. Also, construct the script to rely more
on visual images and responses based on analogies. For
example, you might ask participants to draw a picture of the
ideal service components or to describe the agency's role using
a phrase such as, "the agency is like a bridge because it links
people needing food to the food shelf."

Do all groups need to have the same questions?

Keep the core questions similar across groups so that you can
analyze the responses. Specific groups may have differences
that would make an additional question or two necessary, or
that would require some adjustment in the script.

Worksheets and Samples

Electronic versions of these worksheets may be downloaded from the publisher's web site. Use the following URL to obtain the worksheets

http://www.wilder.org/pubs/workshts/pubs_worksheets1.html?069199

These online worksheets are intended for use in the same way as photocopies of the worksheets, but they are in a form that allows you to type in your responses and reformat the worksheets to fit your focus group. Please do not download the worksheets unless you or your organization has purchased this book.

The first step in developing a focus group is to write a purpose statement that clearly states the goal of your project. Following are some sample purpose statements.

Example 1

A community education program is planning next year's courses and wants to know if it is offering enough daytime classes.

Focus group purpose statement: To find out from community residents their perceptions and ideas about our daytime programming.

Example 2

A mental health agency has greatly expanded its services and wants to revise its mission statement.

Focus group purpose statement: To hear how our constituents perceive and describe our services and to use that information to help us revise our mission statement.

Example 3

A county government is developing a new policy related to its employee benefits and wants to get staff reaction to the draft policy before finalizing it.

Focus group purpose statement: To describe the new benefits policy, find out how staff members feel about it, and write it in language the staff will understand.

Use the following questions to guide the development of your purpose statement.

- What do I want to know?
- Why do I want to know that?
- Is a focus group the best way to get that information?
- Will others understand what I want out of the focus group?

Focus group purpose statement:

✓ = Done	Action	Responsible	By When
☐	1. Write a focus group purpose statement		
☐	2. Identify the participants		
☐	3. Gather address and phone information on the participants		
☐	4. Select a facilitator		
☐	5. Develop the questions		
☐	6. Develop a script		
☐	7. Arrange and reserve the session site		
☐	8. Write and send the invitations		
☐	9. Follow up the invitations with phone calls		
☐	10. Make room arrangements (seating, equipment, refreshments, and so forth)		
☐	11. Place a reminder call to the participants		
☐	12. Gather session materials		
☐	13. Conduct the focus group		
☐	14. Send a thank-you letter to the participants		
☐	15. Transcribe the notes from the session		
☐	16. Summarize the session and mail summary to the participants		
☐	17. Analyze sessions and write a report		

1. Decide how many participants you need and how many you'll need to invite.

   - How many groups will you run? _____

   - How many participants in each group? _____

   - What percentage of invited people will actually attend?_____

   Now use the formula to determine the number of people you will need to invite:

   (number of focus groups) × (number of participants per group)
   ÷ (response rate) = (number of invitations)

   Write the number of invitations you need here: _____

2. Review your focus group purpose statement. Develop a list of key attributes to
   seek in the focus group participants. Write these attributes here.

(continued)

3. Brainstorm possible participants and categories of participants using the list of attributes you developed.

4. Refine the list by using the "two characteristics in common" and the "homogeneity and heterogeneity" guidelines provided on page 18.

5. Secure names and contact information, finalize the list, and send invitations. See the sample invitation on the following page. Remember to mail the invitations three to four weeks before the focus group meets and to make follow-up calls to the registered participants according to the timeline you created in Step 2.

When creating your invitation, be sure to include

☐ A personal invitation (not group) that tells the reader why his or her opinion is important to your organization

☐ The name of the agency sponsoring or conducting the focus group

☐ The date, time, and location, including directions and parking instructions if necessary

☐ The purpose of the focus group

☐ A general statement about who else will be invited

☐ A response form

☐ A response date

☐ A signature by a VIP, such as a neighborhood leader or the executive director of your organization

---

Sample Letter
(put on letterhead)

Date

Malcolm Jones
777 North Street
East St. Paul, MN 55555

Dear Malcolm,

Teen Safe Agency values your role as a leader and decision maker in our community. Because your opinions are important to us, we invite you to participate in a focus group on [date, time, place]. A map and directions are enclosed. The focus group will last about an hour and a half. Refreshments will be served.

Teen Safe is developing a strategic plan to determine its future direction. Through the planning process we want to clarify our role in the community and identify issues that need to be addressed in the coming years. A critical step in this process is to hear from people like you who have an interest in the issues and communities our agency addresses.

I hope you will be able to attend the focus group session so we can hear your thoughts on how Teen Safe can be successful in the next five years and beyond. Please return the response form below to let us know if you will attend.

(continued)

Thank you for your assistance with our plans for the future. Please call me at 555-4321 if you have any questions.

Sincerely

Name, title
Phone

Response Card
(or tear-off sheet)

☐ Yes, I will be able to attend the focus group session on [date, time, place].

☐ Check here if you have any special needs we should plan to accommodate. Please describe:

☐ No, I'm sorry, I will not be able to attend the focus group session.

☐ I am interested in talking with you by phone regarding your plans for the future. Please call me to arrange a time.

Please return this form by [date] to [name, address].

1. Review your purpose statement. Then, on your own or with a group, brainstorm a list of questions.

2. Review the list with the following questions in mind:

   • Are the questions open-ended?
   • Are the questions specific enough?
   • Are there some "warm-up" questions to get the participants ready and comfortable?
   • Will the answers to the questions give me the information I want?

3. Select five or six questions. If using a group, vote on the questions (or use some other method) to arrive at five or six questions.

(continued)

4. Rewrite the questions and organize them into a sequence that will encourage responses from the participants.

5. Test the questions with a pilot group (usually staff from your office).

6. Revise, refine, and retest as needed. When complete, list your questions here:

Use the questions you created in Step 4, along with this sample script, to develop your own script.

OPENING **5 minutes**

1. Facilitator welcomes group and thanks them for coming, then introduces himself or herself and the project and explains the purpose of the focus group.

2. Participants introduce themselves to the rest of the group.

3. Facilitator presents the agenda for the session.

Script: *Welcome to the group, and thank you for joining us. This is one of a series of focus groups that are being conducted to gather information for Teen Safe's strategic planning process. The planning team members hope that by understanding your thoughts about Teen Safe, they can improve their plans. A focus group enables people to come together in one place to share their opinions on a topic. Each of you is representing your own opinions; you do not need to view your comments as representative of an organization or group of people. Please be as honest and open as possible in your responses. Your anonymity will be protected. No one at Teen Safe will know who said what. The results of the focus group will help Teen Safe plan for the future. We will move quickly through a series of questions and should be done in about an hour and a half. Let's start by introducing ourselves.*

WARM-UP **5 minutes**

4. Facilitator takes a quick group survey or temperature gauge. Responses are recorded on an easel after a show of hands.

5. Record this legend on the easel:
   - Very valuable
   - Somewhat valuable
   - Of little value
   - Of no value

Script: *Please comment on how valuable Teen Safe has been in the community using the following scale:*
   - *Very valuable*
   - *Somewhat valuable*
   - *Of little value*
   - *Of no value*

(continued)

QUESTIONS

 15 minutes

6. Facilitator poses Question 1 (strengths). Participants should first record thoughts by themselves on a piece of paper. The facilitator writes comments on a flip chart, taking one comment per person until everyone has had a chance. Continue around the room until all comments are exhausted. Note: Head off destructive exchanges of opinions.

   Script: *What are some specific things about Teen Safe that you think are going well and should definitely be carried into the future?*

 15 minutes

7. Facilitator poses Question 2 (weaknesses). Participants should first record thoughts by themselves on a piece of paper. The facilitator writes comments on the flip chart, taking one comment per person until everyone has had a chance. Continue around the room until all comments are exhausted. Number each comment as it is written on the flip chart. Note: Head off destructive exchanges of opinion. Clarify any comments for yourself or other participants. Combine comments when the entire group agrees that they should be combined.

   Script: *What are some specific things about Teen Safe that you think could be improved in the future?*

 5 minutes

8. Facilitator asks the group to prioritize the list. Everyone gets one-fourth the number of items to vote on. (For example, if the list has twenty-one items, divide the list by four and everyone gets to vote on five items). Record and note top priorities by circling the items with the most votes on the flip chart.

   Script: *If you had to select the four most important areas of improvement to focus on from the entire list that was just generated, which ones would you choose?*

5 minutes

9. Participants are assembled into groups of three. The teams appoint a recorder or reporter. Teams are told to discuss and decide on their top two barriers to making the improvements discussed in Question 8.

   Script: *What are the major barriers to making these improvements?*

  5 minutes

10. The teams report back. Barriers are recorded.

    Script: *Teams, please report back.*

CLOSING   **10 minutes**

11. The facilitator invites the group to note any last thoughts. Additional ideas or emphasis can be turned in separately or participants can call. Facilitator adjourns the session by thanking everyone for their participation and reminds them how the data will be used.

    Script: *Please take out a sheet of paper and note any last thoughts, comments, or things you wish to emphasize for the planning team. You may also call me or any one of the planning team members at [post phone numbers] with comments. Thank you again for your participation. You will receive a summary of this session in the mail. All of the information from this and other focus groups will be reviewed next month and summarized for a planning retreat scheduled for the end of next month. Teen Safe hopes to have a new strategic plan by the beginning of the fiscal year.*

Adapt this example to fit your focus group.

Date of meeting: _____

Arrival time: _____

Start time: _____

Finish time: _____

Focus group purpose statement:

Goals of this focus group:

- To encourage discussion about _____ .
- To hear from other people in the group, exchange ideas, and have face-to-face interaction.
- To create synergy, build off the energy of the group.
- To get more information than can usually be obtained on a written survey.

Group size:

- Number of scheduled participants: _____ .
- If more than twelve people show up, either split into two groups and record the discussions separately or arrange to work in small groups.

Facilitator responsibilities:

- Set the tone: Participants should have fun and feel good about the session.
- Make sure every participant is heard.
- Get full answers (not just "we need more money" but "we need more money to hire a receptionist to answer phones").
- Be sure you understand the written (or recorded) comments.
- Monitor time closely.
- Keep discussion on track.
- Head off destructive exchanges of opinion about individual items.

(continued)

Materials:

☐ Extra notepad and pencils

☐ Flip chart and easel paper

☐ List of participants

☐ Markers

☐ Masking tape

☐ Name tags

☐ Refreshments

☐ Focus group script

☐ Tape recorder (optional)

☐ Watch or clock

Physical setting

- All participants should be able to view one another. (U-shaped seating or all at one table is best.)

- Make sure there are chairs and a writing surface for each participant.

Use this summary sheet to help capture the essence of the focus group and aid in the data analysis.

Facilitator: _____

Date: _____

Focus group: _____

Number of participants: _____

Think:

1. What were the main themes, issues, problems, and questions you witnessed during this session?

2. What people, events, or situations were involved?

3. What were the main themes or issues raised?

4. What new hypotheses, speculations, guesses, or insights related to the focus group purpose statement arose during the session?

5. Are there implications for the next focus group?

6. What happened that was unexpected?

7. What was puzzling?

8. Other comments, reactions, observations?

TEEN SAFE
Staff Focus Group Summary

In December, Teen Safe conducted a focus group of staff to get information pertaining to its strategic planning process. There were twelve participants in the focus group. Information was gathered in four areas: strengths, areas needing improvements, priorities for what should be improved, and major barriers to accomplishing Teen Safe's mission.

Strengths

The focus group participants were asked to name what the agency does well that should be carried on in the future. Below are the topics they mentioned as strengths of the agency:

- Many services available to the community
- Staff relations good
- Staff members work hard
- Record keeping
- Communications with community in general
- Teen Safe is well-known to the public
- Connection with community leaders
- Special events
- Meeting place for clients
- Flexible hours
- Good connection with funders

Improvements

The second question asked, "What could be improved or changed?" After the focus group participants generated a list of improvements, they were each asked to vote for four improvements on which the agency should focus.

The list of improvements follows. The items are listed from most votes to fewest votes, and the number of votes each item received are stated after that item.

- Longer program funding (10)
- Staff training (7)
  - professional training
  - continuing education units
- Better communication (5)
  - staff and management
  - staff and board

(continued)

- Staff benefits (5)
  - retirement or pension
  - raise
- New office space, own a building: new location, more parking (5)
- Visibility and public relations with community (4)
- More diversity on board (4)
- Board and staff should meet once a month (regularly) (3)
- More help to clients (3)
  - expand services beyond social services
- Need to improve incentives to clients (1)
- More staff (1)
- Focus on quality of services, not quantity (1)
- Emotional/behavioral treatment is not of same quality as other interventions
- Fear that Teen Safe will be shut down (1, but facilitator noted nods of agreement from others in room)

Major Barriers to Improvements

The final question asked was, "What are the major barriers to making the improvements discussed in Question 8?" For this discussion, the participants were assembled in groups of three. The groups had five minutes to discuss barriers and pick two. Finally, each group reported its top two barriers. There was overlap between the groups, so the responses were collapsed, with the numbers of groups stating them listed after each statement.

- Inconsistent program funding makes staff feel insecure, makes planning difficult, and damages morale (2)
- Staff members do not have time or incentive to keep up with training (2)
- Lack of clear vision statement and direction from board and top management
- Board does not represent the communities we serve
- Need for frequent communication between units of Teen Safe and with community constituents
- Increasing severity of cases

TEEN SAFE FOCUS GROUPS
Final Report

I. Background and Purpose of the Report

Teen Safe[5] is a residential crisis intervention program for boys and girls ages eleven to seventeen whose behavioral and emotional conditions require round-the-clock supervision. Services include on-site schooling, one-to-one counseling, family crisis intervention, group therapy, communication skills training, health care, and recreational therapy. Clients are referred for a variety of reasons, including self-destructive behavior, sexual acting out, abuse, family crisis, criminal ideation, and anger or aggression control. Teen Safe is located in an older facility in a primarily middle-class residential neighborhood of a large urban area. It has a long and respected history among mental health referral sources, schools, and with city agencies as a whole. Teen Safe is one program at a single site, but is part of a much larger, multisite organization that provides a range of human services to residents of the city.

Teen Safe embarked on a strategic planning process using a private organizational development consultant. As part of the process, a planning team was formed to champion the strategic planning process, assist the consultant in understanding the nuances of the organization, and identify elements critical to its future. This team decided that focus groups would help collect information from staff and some outside stakeholders to guide the strategic plan. The group's stated purpose for the focus group was *to find out what our staff and advisory council see as our greatest strengths and barriers in providing quality services to adolescents.* This report summarizes the information gained from the focus groups.

II. Details of the Focus Group Sessions

Three focus groups were conducted by planning consultant Pat Anser, as outlined below:

Type	Number of People	Session Date
Finance Committee	7	June 6
Staff	10	June 15
Advisory Council	12	July 8

---

[5] This report is based on an actual final report, but details and the name of the organization have been altered.

(continued)

III. Results

There were many common themes expressed across the focus groups as well as several items that surprised the planning team members reviewing the focus group data. These are noted below.

Common Themes

- Funding is limited and becoming more so. It is also inconsistent, making planning difficult and damaging morale.

- The location within a residential community is both a strength and a weakness. Reassuring the neighborhood that Teen Safe is a good neighbor requires extra effort, but the payoffs are excellent. Some felt a new office space was needed.

- Many noted significant staff issues of low pay and frequent turnover.

- Many noted a need for improved communications across all the sites with which Teen Safe is affiliated.

- No one wants to pay for long-term treatment.

- Services are needed for pregnant teens.

- Staff is highly regarded as being caring, dedicated staff who maintain program structure under *high* stress.

- There is a change in the population; children are presenting more difficult problems.

- There is a trend towards correctional and home-based services.

- Teen Safe needs to look for innovative programs.

- Teen Safe should consider preventive residential treatment, such as diversion programs.

- More comprehensive services are needed, including recreation and socialization counseling and services for whole families.

Some representative quotes:

> *"So much is changing with the environment. Less intensive treatment models, more community-based approaches. Managed care and less intensive methodology may mean we have to redefine and strengthen ourselves in new areas."*

"The site is more deeply entrenched in a neighborhood than others. Need to communicate better to the community."

"Sincere desire by staff to be positive change agents."

Surprises

- Comment that we do what's best for staff, not the children (came from one respondent). It seems that at times Teen Safe is more focused on internal issues than on who we are serving and why.

- There seems to be a question of whether Teen Safe would be shut down. It was a surprise that this question arose.

- Teen Safe is viewed by some referring agencies as an extension of county corrections. We didn't know we were perceived this way.

- The emotional-behavioral treatment portion of Teen Safe's services is viewed as being of lower quality than its on-site schooling, family intervention, case management, and other services.

Some representative quotes:

"There is a poor reputation with our treatment program, whereas our shelter program has very good success and large numbers of referrals."

"What if we shut the program down? It seems that the administration is thinking this would be a viable alternative."

IV. Conclusions

The three focus groups highlighted a number of strengths, some areas for improvement, and some significant opportunities. This represents the view of people fairly close to the organization, however. The planning team may need more data about the larger environment to help it determine the best course of action for the next three to five years. Since there seems to be some immediate (and unfounded) concern among the staff that Teen Safe may be shut down, the planning team may want to act now to dispel that rumor and improve communications.

V. Appendix: Focus Group Script

[Not included for this sample. See the Sample Focus Group Script, page 55.]

Helpful Resources

Greenbaum, Thomas L. *The Handbook for Focus Group Research, 2nd Edition, Revised and Expanded.* Thousand Oaks, CA: Sage Publications, 1998.

This book provides an overview of focus groups and their use in marketing research. In addition to basic information on focus groups, the book includes chapters on common mistakes, technology in focus groups, global focus groups, and building a business moderating focus groups. Author Thomas Greenbaum also has a web site (www.groupsplus.com / articles.htm) that features many files of articles he has written on focus groups.

Karger, Ted. "Focus groups are for focusing and for little else." *Marketing News*, 21 (August 28, 1987), 52–55. Published by the American Marketing Association.

The article explores the pros, cons, appropriate, and inappropriate uses of groups to obtain information.

Krueger, Richard A. *Focus Groups: A Practical Guide for Applied Research.* Newbury Park, CA: Sage Publications, 1988.

This is an excellent, easy-to-read book on all you would want to know about focus groups. It explains many aspects of focus groups with some good examples. It does not include worksheets. (Note: a second edition was published in 1994, also by Sage Publications.)

Krueger, Richard A., and David L. Morgan, eds. *The Focus Group Kit* (six volumes). Thousand Oaks, CA: Sage Publications, 1998.

This six-volume set covers focus groups in great detail and may be of great help for consultants or marketing professionals in nonprofits that use focus groups frequently. The titles of the volumes explain the content of the set: The Focus Group Guidebook, Planning Focus Groups, Developing Questions for Focus Groups, Involving Community Members in Focus Groups, Moderating Focus Groups, *and* Analyzing and Reporting Focus Group Results.

Lauer, Larry D. "Are you using the double power of focus groups?" *Nonprofit World*, Volume 14, Number 5 (September/ October 1996) 36–39.

This short article describes what focus groups are and how nonprofits can use them.

Mariampolski, Hy. "Probing correctly uncovers truth behind answers in focus group." *Marketing News*, 22 (October 24, 1988), 22, 26. Published by the American Marketing Association.

The simple article describes different questioning and probing techniques that can be used effectively when conducting focus group sessions.

Templeton, Jane Farley. *Focus Groups: A Guide for Marketing and Advertising Professionals.* Chicago: Probus Publishing Company, 1987.

This 315-page book is aimed at marketing professionals. It is thorough and includes sections on planning, moderating, choosing participants, working with problem groups, writing the final report, and much more.

More results-oriented books from the Amherst H. Wilder Foundation

Collaboration

Collaboration Handbook
Creating, Sustaining, and Enjoying the Journey
by Michael Winer and Karen Ray

Shows you how to get a collaboration going, set goals, determine everyone's roles, create an action plan, and evaluate the results. Includes a case study of one collaboration from start to finish, helpful tips on how to avoid pitfalls, and worksheets to keep everyone on track.

192 pages, softcover   Item # 069032

Collaboration: What Makes It Work, 2nd Ed.
by Paul Mattessich, PhD, Marta Murray-Close, BA, and Barbara Monsey, MPH

An in-depth review of current collaboration research. Major findings are summarized, critical conclusions are drawn, and twenty key factors influencing successful collaborations are identified. Includes The Wilder Collaboration Factors Inventory, which groups can use to assess their collaboration.

104 pages, softcover   Item # 069326

The Nimble Collaboration
Fine-Tuning Your Collaboration for Lasting Success
by Karen Ray

Shows you ways to make your existing collaboration more responsive, flexible, and productive. Provides three key strategies to help your collaboration respond quickly to changing environments and participants.

136 pages, softcover   Item # 069288

Funder's Guides

Community Visions, Community Solutions
Grantmaking for Comprehensive Impact
by Joseph A. Connor and Stephanie Kadel-Taras

Helps foundations, community funds, government agencies, and other grantmakers uncover a community's highest aspiration for itself, and support and sustain strategic efforts to get to workable solutions.

128 pages, softcover   Item # 06930X

Strengthening Nonprofit Performance
A Funder's Guide to Capacity Building
Paul Connolly and Carol Lukas

This practical guide synthesizes the most recent capacity building practice and research into a collection of strategies, steps, and examples that you can use to get started on or improve funding to strengthen nonprofit organizations.

176 pages, softcover   Item # 069377

Management & Planning

The Best of the Board Café
Hands-on Solutions for Nonprofit Boards
by Jan Masaoka, CompassPoint Nonprofit Services

Gathers the most requested articles from the e-newsletter, *Board Café*. You'll find a lively menu of ideas, information, opinions, news, and resources to help board members give and get the most out of their board service.

232 pages, softcover   Item # 069407

Bookkeeping Basics
What Every Nonprofit Bookkeeper Needs to Know
by Debra L. Ruegg and Lisa M. Venkatrathnam

Complete with step-by-step instructions, a glossary of accounting terms, detailed examples, and handy reproducible forms, this book will enable you to successfully meet the basic bookkeeping requirements of your nonprofit organization—even if you have little or no formal accounting training.

128 pages, softcover   Item # 069296

Consulting with Nonprofits: A Practitioner's Guide
by Carol A. Lukas

A step-by-step, comprehensive guide for consultants. Addresses the art of consulting, how to run your business, and much more. Also includes tips and anecdotes from thirty skilled consultants.

240 pages, softcover   Item # 069172

The Wilder Nonprofit Field Guide to Crafting Effective Mission and Vision Statements
by Emil Angelica

Guides you through two six-step processes that result in a mission statement, vision statement, or both. Shows how a clarified mission and vision lead to more effective leadership, decisions, fundraising, and management. Includes tips, sample statements, and worksheets.

88 pages, softcover   Item # 06927X

The Wilder Nonprofit Field Guide to Developing Effective Teams
by Beth Gilbertsen and Vijit Ramchandani

Helps you understand, start, and maintain a team. Provides tools and techniques for writing a mission statement, setting goals, conducting effective meetings, creating ground rules to manage team dynamics, making decisions in teams, creating project plans, and developing team spirit.

80 pages, softcover   Item # 069202

For current prices, a catalog, or to order call ☎ 800-274-6024

The Five Life Stages of Nonprofit Organizations
Where You Are, Where You're Going, and What to Expect When You Get There
by Judith Sharken Simon with J. Terence Donovan

Shows you what's "normal" for each development stage which helps you plan for transitions, stay on track, and avoid unnecessary struggles. This guide also includes The Wilder Nonprofit Life Stage Assessment. The Assessment allows you to plot and understand your organization's progress in seven arenas of organization development.

128 pages, softcover   Item # 069229

The Lobbying and Advocacy Handbook for Nonprofit Organizations
Shaping Public Policy at the State and Local Level
by Marcia Avner

The Lobbying and Advocacy Handbook is a planning guide and resource for nonprofit organizations that want to influence issues that matter to them. This book will help you decide whether to lobby and then put plans in place to make it work.

240 pages, softcover   Item # 069261

The Manager's Guide to Program Evaluation:
Planning, Contracting, and Managing for Useful Results
by Paul W. Mattessich, Ph.D.

Explains how to plan and manage an evaluation that will help identify your organization's successes, share information with key audiences, and improve services.

96 pages, softcover   Item # 069385

The Nonprofit Mergers Workbook
The Leader's Guide to Considering, Negotiating, and Executing a Merger
by David La Piana

A merger can be a daunting and complex process. Save time, money, and untold frustration with this highly practical guide that makes the process manageable and controllable. Includes case studies, decision trees, twenty-two worksheets, checklists, tips, and complete step-by-step guidance from seeking partners to writing the merger agreement, and more.

240 pages, softcover   Item # 069210

Resolving Conflict in Nonprofit Organizations
The Leader's Guide to Finding Constructive Solutions
by Marion Peters Angelica

Helps you identify conflict, decide whether to intervene, uncover and deal with the true issues, and design and conduct a conflict resolution process. Includes exercises to learn and practice conflict resolution skills, guidance on handling unique conflicts such as harassment and discrimination, and when (and where) to seek outside help with litigation, arbitration, and mediation.

192 pages, softcover   Item # 069164

Strategic Planning Workbook for Nonprofit Organizations, Revised and Updated
by Bryan Barry

Chart a wise course for your nonprofit's future. This time-tested workbook gives you practical step-by-step guidance, real-life examples, one nonprofit's complete strategic plan, and easy-to-use worksheets.

144 pages, softcover   Item # 069075

Marketing & Fundraising

The Wilder Nonprofit Field Guide to
Conducting Successful Focus Groups
by Judith Sharken Simon

Shows how to collect valuable information without a lot of money or special expertise. Using this proven technique, you'll get essential opinions and feedback to help you check out your assumptions, do better strategic planning, improve services or products, and more.

80 pages, softcover   Item # 069199

Coping with Cutbacks:
The Nonprofit Guide to Success When Times Are Tight
by Emil Angelica and Vincent Hyman

Shows you practical ways to involve business, government, and other nonprofits to solve problems together. Also includes 185 cutback strategies you can put to use right away.

128 pages, softcover   Item # 069091

The Wilder Nonprofit Field Guide to
Fundraising on the Internet
by Gary M. Grobman, Gary B. Grant, and Steve Roller

Your quick road map to using the Internet for fundraising. Shows you how to attract new donors, troll for grants, get listed on sites that assist donors, and learn more about the art of fundraising. Includes detailed reviews of 77 web sites useful to fundraisers, including foundations, charities, prospect research sites, and sites that assist donors.

64 pages, softcover   Item # 069180

Marketing Workbook for Nonprofit Organizations Volume II: Mobilize People for Marketing Success
by Gary J. Stern

Put together a successful promotional campaign based on the most persuasive tool of all: personal contact. Learn how to mobilize your entire organization, its staff, volunteers, and supporters in a focused, one-to-one marketing campaign. Comes with *Pocket Guide for Marketing Representatives*. In it, your marketing representatives can record key campaign messages and find motivational reminders.

192 pages, softcover   Item # 069105

For current prices or to order visit us online at 🖳 www.wilder.org/pubs

Venture Forth! The Essential Guide to Starting a Moneymaking Business in Your Nonprofit Organization
by Rolfe Larson

The most complete guide on nonprofit business development. Building on the experience of dozens of organizations, this handbook gives you a time-tested approach for finding, testing, and launching a successful nonprofit business venture.

272 pages, softcover   Item # 069245

Vital Communities

Community Building: What Makes It Work
by Wilder Research Center

Reveals twenty-eight keys to help you build community more effectively. Includes detailed descriptions of each factor, case examples of how they play out, and practical questions to assess your work.

112 pages, softcover   Item # 069121

Community Economic Development Handbook
by Mihailo Temali

A concrete, practical handbook to turning any neighborhood around. It explains how to start a community economic development organization, and then lays out the steps of four proven and powerful strategies for revitalizing inner-city neighborhoods.

288 pages, softcover   Item # 069369

The Wilder Nonprofit Field Guide to
Conducting Community Forums
by Carol Lukas and Linda Hoskins

Provides step-by-step instruction to plan and carry out exciting, successful community forums that will educate the public, build consensus, focus action, or influence policy.

128 pages, softcover   Item # 069318

Violence Prevention & Intervention

The Little Book of Peace
Designed and illustrated by Kelly O. Finnerty

A pocket-size guide to help people think about violence and talk about it with their families and friends. You may download a free copy of *The Little Book of Peace* from our web site at www.wilder.org.

24 pages (minimum order 10 copies)   Item # 069083
*Also available in **Spanish** and **Hmong** language editions.*

Journey Beyond Abuse: A Step-by-Step Guide to Facilitating Women's Domestic Abuse Groups
by Kay-Laurel Fischer, MA, LP,
and Michael F. McGrane, LICSW

Create a program where women increase their understanding of the dynamics of abuse, feel less alone and isolated, and have a greater awareness of channels to safety. This book includes twenty-one group activities that you can combine to create groups of differing length and focus.

208 pages, softcover   Item # 069148

Moving Beyond Abuse: Stories and Questions for Women Who Have Lived with Abuse
(Companion guided journal to *Journey Beyond Abuse*)

A series of stories and questions that can be used in coordination with the sessions provided in the facilitator's guide or with the guidance of a counselor in other forms of support.

88 pages, softcover   Item # 069156

Foundations for Violence-Free Living:
A Step-by-Step Guide to Facilitating Men's Domestic Abuse Groups
by David J. Mathews, MA, LICSW

A complete guide to facilitating a men's domestic abuse program. Includes twenty-nine activities, detailed guidelines for presenting each activity, and a discussion of psychological issues that may arise out of each activity.

240 pages, softcover   Item # 069059

On the Level
(Participant's workbook to *Foundations for Violence-Free Living*)
Contains forty-nine worksheets including midterm and final evaluations. Men can record their progress.

160 pages, softcover   Item # 069067

What Works in Preventing Rural Violence
by Wilder Research Center

An in-depth review of eighty-eight effective strategies you can use to prevent and intervene in violent behaviors, improve services for victims, and reduce repeat offenses. This report also includes a Community Report Card with step-by-step directions on how you can collect, record, and use information about violence in your community.

94 pages, softcover   Item # 069040

For current prices, a catalog, or to order call ☎ 800-274-6024

ORDERING INFORMATION

Order by phone, fax or online

Call toll-free: 800-274-6024
Internationally: 651-659-6024

Fax: 651-642-2061

E-mail: books@wilder.org
Online: www.wilder.org/pubs

Mail: Amherst H. Wilder Foundation
Publishing Center
919 Lafond Avenue
St. Paul, MN 55104

Our NO-RISK guarantee

If you aren't completely satisfied with any book for any reason, simply send it back within 30 days for a full refund.

Pricing and discounts

For current prices and discounts, please visit our web site at www.wilder.org/pubs or call toll free at 800-274-6024.

Do you have a book idea?

Wilder Publishing Center seeks manuscripts and proposals for books in the fields of nonprofit management and community development. To get a copy of our author guidelines, please call us at 800-274-6024. You can also download them from our web site at www.wilder.org/pubs/author_guide.html.

Visit us online

You'll find information about the Wilder Foundation and more details on our books, such as table of contents, pricing, discounts, endorsements, and more, at www.wilder.org/pubs.

Quality assurance

We strive to make sure that all the books we publish are helpful and easy to use. Our major workbooks are tested and critiqued by experts before being published. Their comments help shape the final book and—we trust—make it more useful to you.